A BEAR'S TALE

A Science-based Short Story for Young Readers

by

G. Michael Schenck

Age Group Editor – Skyler Dykes

Photography by Bernard "Bud" Marschner

For Justin

*For Madalynn, Ryan, Jonah
and Keaton*

For Skyler, Tayler and Cooper

Thanks for technical assistance from:

Darrin Schenck
Kristle Schulz
Mike Wong

A
BEAR'S TALE

It is winter on a far away mountain. The peaks lay covered in snow. A female black bear is snug in her small, warm den. She has been hibernating for nearly three months. Her last walk on the nearby ridge took place at the end of October.

With the first signs of winter, the bear began looking for a den. This year she has chosen an old cave. The cave is near the top of the mountain where the snow will hide it. The den has only a small opening. The living space inside is not much larger than the bear. The bear must have believed she had found a perfect location.

To prepare the den, her first step had been to clean house. She removed rocks and sticks that littered the den floor. Next, she carried mouthfuls of grass and leaves into the den to create a soft, warm bed. When she finally entered for a long winter snooze, she had enough dry leaves to close the opening of the cave. This would keep out the freezing weather. In the den, she would stay warm all winter long.

Now, she sleeps. She may even dream bear dreams. Human scientists aren't sure. Perhaps she dreams of stealing a tasty deer that a young mountain lion had killed. Perhaps she is dreaming of trips to a summer berry patch and all of the blueberries she will eat. Or, maybe she is thinking of catching a fat fish from the stream in the canyon below.

Bears hibernate when the temperature is cold and there is little food. *Hibernation* is like being in a very deep sleep. Some bears hibernate for six months of the year.

She snoozes through the blizzard just outside her door. But she is aware of an important event that is about to take place. New

copyright Bernard Marschner 2007

life began growing inside her in early July. Within days now, in about the third week of January, a litter of cubs will come into the world.

This will be the mother bear's third litter. She has been a successful mother. She had given birth to her first cub when she was four years old. Two years later, two more cubs were born. She was very good at teaching her cubs the things they needed to know to survive in the wild. During their second summer, mama made each of them find their own home so she could begin another new family.

The mother bear is eight years old. She is large for a female black bear. She weighs almost 250 pounds. She is very wise about living in the woods. Few other creatures would want to cross her path.

Today is a special day. The bear has to wake up. It is time for her cubs to be born. Like thousands of bears before her, she brings three tiny new lives into her small den. She checks each one with a good sniffing. She licks each of them clean. Being born is messy. Soon she can hear the sound of tiny squeals and whimpers. Then she drifts off for a few more weeks of sleep.

The new cubs do not hibernate. These three tiny creatures hardly seem like they will one day be mighty bears. They can't see at all just after they are born. They can't hear sounds either. They can't smell anything for a while. They are covered with short, fuzzy hair. Each of the cubs weighs only one half pound. In the outside world, even a gray squirrel would be as tall as one of these tiny, helpless babies.

But the young cubs grow at a fast rate. Mother bear's milk is very rich. Healthy cubs gain as much as one pound a week. By

the time mother is ready to leave her den, the three furry bundles will weigh as much as ten pounds each.

The mother bear sleeps for another eight weeks. Finally, there are several days of warm temperatures. Melting snow begins to drip into the den. The mother bear becomes wide awake. She knows it is the time to end her hibernation. She must go back to her normal activities. She must begin to teach her cubs how to be bears. In a few days, she will leave the den for good. She will probably never use this den again.

Now in early June, the mother and cubs have moved to the outside world. For a short time, mother takes shelter in a dense thicket near the den. There is good cover and fresh water. Here she can protect her cubs from *predators*. Wolves and bobcats and other adult bears are predators. They would catch and eat a tender young cub. Mother needs time to allow her body to adjust. After all, she has been asleep for over five months.

In about two weeks, the bear family begins to travel down into the valley. Everything is new to the cubs. They stop to investigate butterflies. They chase after a frog. They find a patch of snow on a shady hill and play slide. Mother has to be very patient.

When they reach the valley floor, it is warm and green. This is where they will spend the summer and fall. This area is the mother bear's *home range*. It has everything the bears will need. There is cool water. There is dense cover. There is plenty of the foods bears like best.

Other bears have a home range, too. Some of them are near the mother bear's territory. Her first cub lives in a home range just

over the ridge. Usually only one male bear lives in the area. He will fight with other male bears to keep them away. When breeding season comes, he will find the mother bear. This time of year, she will stay far away from the big old male. She knows he will kill her cubs if he can catch them.

The family spends its days roaming throughout the valley. They spend much of their time eating. Eating is a bear's favorite activity. They will eat whatever nature has to offer. Bears eat both plants and meat. The name for animals that eat both plants and meat is *omnivorous*.

But there is also time for other things. Cubs are very playful. They are always into something. They splash in the cool stream. Bears love to swim. They climb trees. Bears are excellent climbers. They wrestle and play tag. It helps them grow stronger.

There are lessons to be learned, too. One morning is spent digging on a hillside for tasty roots like wild onion. On another afternoon, mother will show how to turn over rocks along the stream to find crayfish. On a warm summer evening, the family will be found nibbling on not-quite-ripe blueberries.

One day, the group finds a bee hive hidden in the trunk of a hollow tree. Mother climbs to the hive. She knows about the delicious golden honey. Bears have the most excellent noses. They can smell food better than most other animals, even a dog. Before long, the cubs have sniffed out the treat. They enjoy the honey, too. The bees don't like the bears breaking into their hive and eating their honey. They are angry. They sting and sting the bears. The mother bear doesn't seem to mind the stinging. The cubs climb down and run away from the bees.

The young bears learn quickly in this green valley. Each has begun to develop its own personality. The male cub is larger than his sisters. He is the bravest of the cubs. He gets into trouble by not obeying his mother. Then she gives him a swat with one of her large front paws. He likes to hide and pretend to attack his sisters. Sometimes they fight back and sometimes they run away from him.

One of his sisters has a brown coat. She is the "mama's baby" of the group. She is never far from her mother's side. She pays attention to all of her lessons. She is the smallest cub.

The other sister is black. She looks like a smaller version of her mother. She's not so afraid as her little sister. She's not as brave as her bigger brother. She is very curious. She sticks her nose and paws into all kinds of holes. Once a raccoon bit her on the nose.

The bear family spends the summer traveling throughout their beautiful valley. The cubs are learning about the other forest animals. They see deer and rabbits. A gray fox lives in the valley, too. There are robins and blue jays and crows. Most animals are afraid of the bears.

One day the cubs smell a strong odor in the air. Humans would say it is a terrible smell. To the bears, it smells delicious. Carried by the wind is the scent of a dead elk.

The old elk was too weak after a hard winter. He died by the stream. When the bears find the elk, they have meat to eat for several days. Soon there is nothing remaining but bones. The old elk has helped the bears to live.

copyright Bernard Marschner 2007

Later in the summer, the family is traveling along a trail. Suddenly, mother bear becomes very nervous. She can smell a strange bear nearby. The cubs can smell him, too. They are frightened and press close by mother's side. Mother bear turns to go but it is too late!

From out of the bushes rushes a large male bear. He is nearly twice as big as the mother. He growls and runs at the cubs. They see his sharp teeth. They know he wants to hurt them. They run for the nearest tree as fast as little paws can carry them.

The big old male is very fast. Mother can see her cubs will not get away. Faster than any human can run, the mother charges her enemy. She has to save her babies! She will fight the male bear if necessary.

The big male sees her coming. He knows she is very angry. He tries to stop and turn around. Instead, he does a summersault across the trail. When he lands, mother is nearly on top of him. He tries to jump out of the way. She grabs his ear in her teeth and bites hard. The big bear lets out a loud bawl. When he breaks loose, a piece of his ear is torn. He runs away into the bushes.

Mother bear chases after him only a few steps. She does not want to go into the thick brush where he can surprise her. She returns to her frightened youngsters. By now, they have climbed to the very top of a tall pine tree. Even big brother is not so brave now. Mother gives the command to come down. Quickly, all three cubs are at her side. They have learned that they must stay ever alert.

Bears know instinctively they must grow fat to survive the winter. While other forest animals suffer through freezing weather, bears are sound asleep. They use their body fat to live. To get really fat, the bears must spend most of their time eating, especially in the fall. Fall is when bears mostly eat acorns. Acorns help them grow fat and healthy. Acorns grow on oak trees. One day, the family climbs high up on the ridge to the old oak trees. They find acorns everywhere. They walk along a well-worn trail and nibble on sweet acorns. They don't even have to climb the trees to find them. The wind has blown the acorns to the ground.

Suddenly, mother can smell something coming along the trail. Now she can hear voices, too. A group of hikers is coming around a bend. The hikers are laughing and talking. At first, they don't see the bears. When they do, they stand frozen in their tracks. They are afraid. The humans have heard stories about bears attacking people. They don't know what the big mother bear plans to do.

The cubs are frightened, too. They have never before seen people. They don't know what to make of these strange creatures walking on two legs.

Mother has seen humans before. She has seen them hiking. She has seen them catching fish from the stream. Those humans had been less alert. They didn't see her and she had always sneaked away.

Now she isn't sure what to do. The humans are very close to her cubs. Do they plan to hurt the cubs?

copyright Bernard Marschner 2007

Each group looks at the other. Each wonders what is going to happen next. Finally, mother bear makes a decision. She turns off the trail. She and her cubs sneak away in thick cover. Like most black bears, she does not want trouble with humans. She just wants to be able to do the things bears do. She is willing to share the mountain.

When the bears disappear, the hikers feel better. What an exciting story they have to tell around the campfire. They learned black bears are not so dangerous if they are left alone. The cubs learned, too. They learned what people are. They learn it is best to avoid people when they come around.

The days are growing shorter now. Summer is changing to fall. Leaves are coming off the trees. Mornings are turning frosty. The bear family is fat and healthy. The mother knows it will soon be time to look for a den. She will need a bigger den this year. This time, the three cubs will share the space with her.

When the snow flurries come, she goes high into the mountains. By the time the first snow storm arrives, the family is snug in bed. No matter how cold it gets outside, they will be warm and safe in the den. Winter for them will be like one long night's sleep. November turns into December and the family sleeps. January comes and goes. Still they sleep. February ….. March ….. April….., they snooze away. Once in a while, one of the bears will wake up. But what is there to do? They look around the dark den. Then they roll over and go back to sleep. It just takes too much energy to stay awake.

Finally, on a warm day in May, the bears wake up. They move slowly. They have to stretch after such a long sleep. They yawn and scratch. All of the bears are thin and hungry. They haven't had anything to eat or drink for almost six months!

Once again, mother takes them down from the mountain and into the valley. She can see her three cubs look different now. Even though they have slept all winter, they have grown bigger and taller. They are no longer babies.

Soon the family is munching on fresh green grass and dandelions and other tender spring plants. They take long drinks of the cool, sweet water. Mother takes them to a favorite hill. Here, she knows they can dig up roots to eat. They have big appetites. As the days pass, the bears begin to add pounds. Once again, they are a healthy, active family.

Mother continues to teach lessons. The youngsters have learned many things about the ways of bear life. Although they are young, they are almost ready to live on their own. Mother knows that time is coming soon.

For the next six weeks, the family travels through their wonderful valley. They visit familiar places. They eat favorite foods. They eat and eat and eat. The cubs are always hungry. They are growing fast. The male cub is now much larger than his sisters.

As the days grow longer, the bears begin to look shaggy. They are losing their beautiful winter coats. They are too hot in the warm sunshine. Summer hair is growing in. The old hair makes the cubs itch. They will rub their sides against rocks. They will stand up and rub their backs against a tree trunk. They rub in the dirt and on the bushes. They even rub against each other. Soon, their new coat is short and sleek.

copyright Bernard Marschner 2007

One day, the group finds the trail of a male bear. The cubs stop. They remember the last time they ran into a male bear. They are nervous. But this time, mother acts differently. Instead of taking them away, she just sniffs at the trail. She doesn't follow but she doesn't appear afraid.

Several days later, the family again smells the male bear. This time, mother bear follows along his trail a short distance. Now, she seems to want to find the male. A change is taking place.

Later that day, mother chases the three cubs away before she eats a fresh fish. This is the first time she doesn't want to share. When they return to her, she pays little attention to them. That night, she and the cubs don't sleep together as a group.

The cubs can't understand. But mother knows breeding season is near. She knows it is almost time to create a new family. She also knows her cubs will be in danger if a male bear comes to join her.

So, early the next morning, mother bear says goodbye to her cubs. It is time for them to go out and find their own homes. But they don't want to leave. She chases them away but they come right back. In order to convince them, she finally bites at the rear of one of her cubs. Now they understand. They must go.

The cubs are sad to leave their mother. They have never been on their own before. They walk through the woods together for the rest of the day. They call for the mother bear. She won't come. That night, the three cubs sleep together in a large tree.

copyright Bernard Marschner

They spend the next few days together, too. One day, the male cub decides to go off on his own. The sisters never see him again after that. A few days later, the sisters go different ways, too. Each of the young bears goes off to find a new home range.

The sisters do not have to travel far. They stay near the mother's territory. There is lots of food and plenty of room. The male cub is chased off by a bigger bear. He has several fights with other males. Finally, he finds a safe home on the other side of the mountain.

Each of the cubs has learned its lessons well. There are many dangers but they know how to take care of themselves. The old mother bear has been a good teacher. The cubs will grow to be adults. They will produce families of their own.

Later, when the weather turns cold, the mother bear walks back up the mountain to find a den. When the first snow storm comes, it covers the door of her den. But she is inside, sound asleep. Days and weeks pass by.

She snoozes through the harsh blizzard just outside. But she is aware of the important event that will soon take place. It is almost the third week in January once again. In just a few days, a new pair of fuzzy little babes will join her. She'll no longer be alone. The bear's tale will go on.

About the Author …

Michael Schenck is a life-long outdoors enthusiast and conservationist. A native of Pennsylvania, he had his first encounter with a black bear on one of the Keystone State's isolated trout streams. It would create an interest that became a passion and an avocation. In 1984, he relocated to Phoenix, Arizona after falling in love with the state's wide open spaces and unspoiled habitat. He currently resides in Arizona with his wife, Arleen.

In 1986, Mr. Schenck joined a small group of sportsmen to form the North American Bear Society (N.A.B.S.). In 1995, he became President/CEO of the group which had gained notoriety as an international conservation organization. Mr. Schenck has also served as the Chief Administrative Officer of the Arizona Wildlife Federation and as President of the Arizona Black Bear Association.

copyright Bernard Marschner 2007

About the Photographer …

Bernard "Bud" Marschner is an amateur photographer living in Fairbanks, Alaska with his wife, Jamie.

Bud's unique ability to capture the wildlife and landscape of the "Last Frontier" has produced the exceptional images provided with this story. The Marschners have spent many enjoyable hours in observation of bears at the Anan Creek Wildlife Observatory, near Wrangell, AK, where these photos were taken, and at McNeil River Falls (pictured below) in the McNeil River State Game Refuge southwest of Anchorage, AK.

copyright Bernard Marschner 2008

Interesting Facts About The
North American Black Bear

- Approximately 800,000 black bears live in North America.
- Black Bears are not endangered. There are more black bears today than ever before.
- Black bears live in 42 of the United States.
- Canada has the largest population of black bears.
- Some black bears live in the mountains of northern and central Mexico.
- Male black bears usually weigh 200 to 400 pounds. They can grow much larger.
- Female black bears are usually smaller than males. They weigh between 125 and 250 pounds.
- A mother bear can have from one to six cubs in a litter.
- A black bear cub weighs only one half pound at birth.
- Black bears can live to be 20 to 30 years old.
- A black bear has a great sense of smell, even better than a dog.
- Black bears hibernate for up to six months of the year. This helps them avoid cold temperatures and a lack of food in winter.
- Black bears are extremely strong and very intelligent.
- Black bears will eat just about anything. They eat natural foods like plants, berries and fish. They also love the same foods people enjoy and they eat garbage.
- Black bears don't often attack people. But they can be very dangerous. People should leave bears alone.